Journal

The Teachings of Michael

By
Robert P Theiss

This JOURNAL belongs to:

_____

The Teachings of Michael

Living inside every human being is a very simple truth: Spirit is deeply in love with you. Spirit has never withheld its love from any aspect of life. This presence is very sincere about the nature of love. It is and has always been unconditional. Spirit demands nothing from life; it has no expectations or agendas. It never worries, doubts, or has any concerns about how we choose to represent our own unique consciousness. Spirit offers such a pure and simple relationship that we often refuse to believe it's real.

Reconnecting with our divine nature is perhaps the most empowering experience any human being will ever have. A spiritual awakening is unique to each person but I believe there are stages and symptoms within the awakening process that we can identify and use as a guide.

The teachings of Michael represent a universal perspective that supports the awakening process. Journal writing can serve this new relationship by helping us to reconnect with our soul as we explore our thoughts and beliefs, embrace our dreams and aspirations. We invite you to embrace a new relationship with Spirit with a renewed sense of compassion, integrity and joy.

Awakening Symptoms

· Physical

Our bodies have the ability to store experiences from our past in our DNA. Shifting our attention to being in the moment helps to release energies that no longer serve us. It is common to experience during this transition a variety of physical discomforts. Breathing, mild exercise, and drinking large amounts of water can ease this transition. Many people experience feeling ungrounded, lightheaded, or disconnected from their body. Spend a day at the coast, in the mountains, or in a desert. Sitting with your back next to a tree can be very helpful. You can also imagine that your body has a taproot that extends down from the base of your spine into the center of the Earth. Your diet will naturally change to accommodate your new relationship with yourself. Begin to trust that your body has its own intelligence and is working overtime to integrate your growing awareness. What, when, and how you eat can change on a daily basis. Pay attention to how your body feels after each meal.

· **Emotions**

It is normal in any awakening process to experience a full spectrum of emotions. One day you might feel you're on top of the world, full of energy, enthusiasm, and joy. Twenty-four hours later, it might take every ounce of energy just to crawl out of bed. It's important that you learn to observe your emotions from a sovereign heart and mind and allow all of these feelings to surface. Trust, acceptance, and a very good sense of humor will ease this transition.

· **Mental**

The mind has been leading the soul around on a leash for a long time. Changing this relationship requires a lot of patience. As you begin to shift using your past to define your identity, it is common to have short-term memory loss. Living in the present moment has no history attached to it. Your mind becomes a witness to your new experiences as it gathers information to re-create your identity. This is a very frustrating experience for the mind; it feels like your story is dissolving, but that's only because it is! Integrating new choices into your life takes time. As you begin to embrace a new, sovereign identity, you will need to teach your mind how to serve that relationship.

· **Spiritual**

The awakening process naturally triggers a deep desire to return to the source of life. This long-held yearning has been with you throughout all of creation. You can now fulfill this desire by allowing Spirit to come to you. The art of being in receivership transforms our relationship with Spirit, our God Self, and all of life.

· **Relationships**

A self-empowered human being can challenge all of our personal relationships. Be gentle and patient with yourself, knowing you are not responsible for how others feel. Over time, new friends and companions will enter your life that honor and respect your new choices.

· **Employment**

A spiritual awakening invites us to place a greater value on our self. We begin to embrace a new freedom to express all of our heartfelt desires. This naturally changes how we feel about our work environment. You will discover new opportunities that will support your growing awareness.

· **Creativity**

In the past, our passion for life was fueled by pursuing, achieving, and setting goals and fulfilling predetermined agendas. This required a lot of hard work and effort. As you become accustomed to living in the moment, you will discover a new passion that is supported by a sovereign heart and mind. You will discover the freedom to express yourself outside the conditions and parameters you inherited.

A spiritual awakening embraces change, but all of these symptoms will pass in time, and you will look back at all the choices you were willing to make for yourself with a deep sense of appreciation and joy.

Physical

Emotional

Mental

Spiritual

Relationships

Employment

Creativity

A New Story

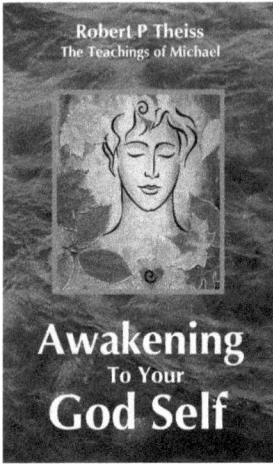

Awakening to your God Self
Paperback / ISBN: 978-0-578-07815-1
147 pages $14.95
Published by Ancient Wings®
A Spiritual Handbook

www.ancientwings.com

www.ingramcontent.com/pod-product-compliance
Lightning Source LLC
Chambersburg PA
CBHW070842100426

42813CB00003B/718